G000167133

# Drama for Students, Volume 16

**Project Editor**: David Galens

**Editorial**: Anne Marie Hacht, Michelle Kazensky, Ira Mark Milne, Pam Revitzer, Kathy Sauer, Timothy J. Sisler, Jennifer Smith, Carol Ullmann

**Research**: Sarah Genik

**Permissions**: Kim Davis, Debra Freitas

**Manufacturing**: Stacy Melson

**Imaging and Multimedia**: Lezlie Light, Dave Oblender, Kelly A. Quin, Luke Rademacher

**Product Design**: Pamela A. E. Galbreath, Michael Logusz

*For more information, contact*

ISBN 0-7876-6031-0

Printed in the United States of America
10 9 8 7 6 5 4 3

# Cloud Nine

Caryl Churchill 1979

## Introduction

*Cloud Nine,* by British playwright Caryl Churchill, was first performed at Dartington College of Arts in February 1979 by the Joint Stock Theatre Group. It was then performed on tour at the Royal Court Theatre in London and was first staged in New York in 1981.

*Cloud Nine,* which can be found in Churchill's *Plays One*(London and New York, 1985), was a popular and critical success. In addition to frequently being very amusing, the play highlights colonial and gender oppression. The first act is set in the nineteenth century in an African country ruled by Britain, and Churchill satirizes the repressive nature of the Victorian family, the rigidity of narrowly prescribed gender roles, and the phenomenon whereby oppressed peoples in colonized countries take on the identity of the colonizers. Act two takes place in London one hundred years later with mostly the same characters, who have aged only twenty-five years. In this act, Churchill explores such topics as women's liberation, gay liberation, and the sexual revolution, all of which were prominent social movements in Britain, as well as the United States, in the 1970s.

# Author Biography

Caryl Churchill was born on September 3, 1938, in London, England. She spent most of her early childhood in and near London before her family moved in 1948 to Montreal, Canada, where Churchill attended the Trafalgar School until 1955. Churchill began to write as a young girl, and she also developed an early interest in the theater. She continued these interests during her undergraduate years, which began in 1957 when she enrolled at Lady Margaret Hall, Oxford, in England. She graduated with a Bachelor of Arts in English in 1960. During her university years, two of her plays received student productions, and in 1962, *The Ants,* her first professional radio play, was broadcast.

In 1961, she married David Harter, a barrister, and from 1963 to 1969 the couple had three sons. During this period Churchill continued to write radio plays, including *Identical Twins*(1968), and to develop a socialist and feminist approach to drama. Churchill's first professional stage production was *Owners,* performed at the Royal Court Theatre Upstairs in London in 1972. The play premiered in New York the following year. During the 1970s, Churchill wrote a number of plays that were broadcast on BBC television, including *Turkish Delight*(1974) and *The After-Dinner Joke*(1978). Her two stage plays, *Objections to Sex and Violence*(1975) and *Light Shining in Buckinghamshire*(1976), brought her critical attention. The latter play was the result of Churchill's involvement in London's experimental Joint Stock Theatre Group. Another play written for Joint Stock was *Cloud Nine,* which in 1979 became Churchill's first big success. It was also a hit in the United States, where it opened off-Broadway in New York at the Theatre de Lys in May 1981 to positive reviews and large audiences. *Cloud Nine* won the Obie Award in 1982.

Churchill followed this success with *Top Girls,* a play that portrays women achieving success by imitating the worst of male behaviors. It was staged at Royal Court Theatre in 1982 and transferred to New York later that year. It also won an Obie Award. In 1983, Churchill wrote *Fen,* which was the result of a group of Joint Stock actors and playwrights living for two weeks in a hard-pressed farming community in the Fens of England. *Fen* was a critical and popular success in London and New York, and it won the 1984 Susan Smith Blackburn Prize.

After *Softcops*(1984), which was performed by the Royal Shakespeare Company in London, and *A Mouthful of Birds*(1986), co-written with David Lan, Churchill wrote *Serious Money*(1987), a play about greed and financial scandal on London's stock exchange. Two short plays followed, *Ice Cream* and *Hot Fudge*(1989), and then *Mad Forest*(1990), in which Churchill examined life in Romania before, during, and after the downfall of the dictator Nicolae Ceausescu. During the 1990s, Churchill wrote *Lives of the Great Poisoners*(1991);

the surreal and mythic *The Skriker*(1994); *Thyestes*(1994), a translation of a play by Seneca; *Hotel*(1997), in which all the parts are sung; and *This Is a Chair*(1999).

# Act 1, Scene 1

Act 1 of *Cloud Nine* is set in a British African colony in the nineteenth century. The first scene takes place on the verandah of a house. After an opening song introduces the characters, Clive tells his wife, Betty, that he is expecting a visitor, Harry Bagley, an explorer. Betty tells Clive that their black servant, Joshua, insulted her, and Clive makes Joshua apologize. Then the family gathers: their children Victoria and Edward; the governess, Ellen; and Betty's mother, Maud. Edward is looking after Victoria's doll, which annoys his father because he thinks this is unmasculine. Betty is nervous at the thought of entertaining a guest. Mrs. Saunders, a widowed neighbor, arrives to take shelter; the local tribes are preparing for war, and she is afraid to stay in her own house. Harry arrives, and he and Clive speak about the dangerous situation, exhibiting a disdainful view of the indigenous people. Harry and Betty are left alone; they are romantically attracted to each other. The scene ends as Harry, who is bisexual, propositions Joshua for sex.

# Act 1, Scene 2

A couple of nights later, in an open space some distance from the house, Mrs. Saunders meets with Clive. It is revealed that Clive has already seduced her and has a sexual passion for her, which she goes along with even though she does not like him.

The family gathers for a Christmas picnic. They play a ball game, but the men monopolize it, claiming that the women cannot catch. Then everyone plays hide and seek. Joshua warns Clive that the stable boys are not reliable and are carrying knives. Harry and Betty exchange endearments, and Betty bemoans the fact that they can never be alone. Edward says he loves Harry, and it is clear that they have on former occasions had sex with each other. Betty confides in Ellen that she loves Harry, and Ellen reveals that she is in love with Betty.

## *Act 1, Scene 3*

In the house, the women discuss the fact that the stable boys are being flogged, and Mrs. Saunders goes to investigate the situation. Edward is still fond of Victoria's doll, but Betty takes it away from him and slaps him, and Ellen slaps him also. Edward confesses to the returning Clive that he said bad things about his father, but Clive forgives him because he owned up. Clive reveals that he knows of Betty's feelings for Harry and is ready to forgive her, but he says she must resist her lustful feelings or they will destroy their marriage.

## *Act 1, Scene 4*

On the verandah, Clive tells of a raid by British soldiers on a nearby village. Edward pleads with

Harry to stay, while Ellen says she only wants to be with Betty forever. Clive tells Harry that he values male friendship; Harry misinterprets this and makes a sexual advance, which disgusts Clive, who tells Harry that he must save himself by marrying. Mrs. Saunders informs Clive that Joshua's parents were killed in the British raid, but when Clive offers him a day off, Joshua sides with the British, saying his parents were bad people. Harry proposes marriage to Mrs. Saunders, who is not interested, and then to Ellen.

## *Act 1, Scene 5*

On the verandah, there is a wedding reception for Harry and Ellen. Ellen confesses to Betty that she knows nothing about lovemaking, but Betty says there is nothing to it. Mrs. Saunders announces that she is leaving the next day, and Clive kisses her, which prompts Betty to lunge at her in a jealous assault. Clive blames Mrs. Saunders and says she must leave instantly. After her departure, Harry makes a speech, the wedding cake is cut, and then Clive makes a speech also, congratulating the couple and saying that all is well. But at that moment, Joshua readies himself to shoot Clive. Edward sees this but does nothing to alert the others.

## *Act 2, Scene 1*

This scene takes place one hundred years later on a winter afternoon in a London park. Some of the characters from act one reappear, but they are only twenty-five years older. Victoria is married to Martin, and they have a son, Tommy. Victoria's friend Lin, who is divorced, has a four-year-old girl, Cathy. Cathy plays with a gun as the two women talk about the problems of parenting; Lin says that she is a lesbian and hates men. Edward, who is a gardener at the park, arrives and tells Victoria that their mother is walking there. This is not good news for Victoria, since she does not like her mother. Betty appears with Tommy, who has a bruise from playing rough games. Betty announces that she is going to leave Clive. When Betty leaves, Edward and Victoria express their surprise and consternation, believing that now, both their parents will need a lot of attention. As the scene ends, Lin propositions Victoria for sex.

## *Act 2, Scene 2*

In the spring, Edward and his gay lover Gerry are outside in the open air. Edward seeks an explanation of where Gerry was the previous night, but Gerry is evasive. After Edward leaves, Gerry tells of his sexual adventures in a soliloquy. Victoria and Betty talk. Betty says she is worried that she will not be able to manage on her own, now that she has left Clive. She is frightened. Martin tries to offer Victoria support in her dilemma about whether to accept a job in Manchester, but his advice is not much use to her because he is more concerned with demonstrating how good and understanding he is than with helping her. Lin is in love with Victoria and asks her to live with her. Then Lin reveals that her brother, a British soldier, has been killed that morning in Belfast, Northern Ireland. Gerry tells Edward he is bored with their relationship, which is too much like that between husband and wife. Gerry says he is moving out of the apartment they share. Edward expresses amorous interest in his sister, touching her breasts, and she does not object.

## *Act 2, Scene 3*

In the park on a summer night, Victoria, Lin, and Edward are drunk. They perform a farcical ceremony in preparation for a sexual orgy. Martin arrives, and the three of them jump on him and try to make love to him. They are interrupted by a stranger who turns out to be Lin's dead brother, Bill, who is there because he wants sex. As the others leave, Gerry arrives on his own and tells the audience how he picks up lovers in the park. Then all the characters sing a song called Cloud Nine, which is an expression for sexual ecstasy.

## *Act 2, Scene 4*

It is an afternoon in late summer. Lin, Edward, and Victoria now live together along with the two children. Betty arrives and announces that she has a job as a doctor's receptionist and enjoys it. When Betty, Lin, and Victoria leave, Gerry arrives. Edward tells him that he is now unemployed and that in his new domestic situation, he does the housework. Gerry tells him of another sexual adventure; they arrange to meet for a meal. When they leave, Betty returns and tells of her sexual awakening. Victoria reveals that she has decided to go to Manchester. After she leaves, Betty befriends Gerry and invites him to dinner. She says she knows that both her son and Gerry are gay and that this does not distress her. Then Clive appears for the first time since act one and says that he does not feel the same way about Betty that he used to. He also bemoans the loss of the British Empire. Finally, Betty from act one enters, and she and Betty from act two embrace.

## *Harry Bagley*

Harry Bagley is an explorer and a friend of Clive. Clive regards him as an eccentric—a bit of a poet as well as a hothead. Betty says he is a bore and a heavy drinker, but when Harry visits Clive and his family, she falls in love with him because he kisses her and says he needs her. However, Harry is bisexual, and his main interest appears to be males of any description. It is revealed that on a previous visit he seduced Edward, and he also propositions Joshua and Clive. Clive is horrified by this and tells Harry he must marry. So, to keep up the appearance of propriety, Harry marries Ellen.

## *Betty*

Betty is Clive's wife and is played by a man. Betty accepts her role as the dutiful Victorian wife, living only for her husband. But she finds her life monotonous and boring. When Harry arrives, she allows herself to develop a passion for him, which Clive, who finds out about it through Joshua, tells her she must overcome. Betty's unfaithfulness, however, does not prevent her from becoming jealous when Clive kisses Mrs. Saunders.

In act two, Betty reappears and is twenty-five years older. This time she is played by a woman.

She has decided to leave her husband, and at first she has difficulty building an independent life for herself. But she finds her feet when she gets a job as a receptionist in a doctor's office. She also learns to explore her own sexuality through masturbation. She no longer lives entirely for and through a man.

## *Cathy*

Cathy is the four-year-old daughter of Lin. She is played by a man. In the park, Cathy amuses herself by painting and playing with guns, and she also likes to play with a group of boys called the Dead Hand Gang. But she has refused to wear jeans at school since the other children called her a boy. She now wears only dresses.

## *Clive*

Clive is a British colonial administrator, married to Betty. He is a loyal, patriotic servant of the British Empire, and he has a patronizing and sometimes brutal attitude toward the local Africans, whom he does not trust. Clive is soaked in Victorian moral values. He takes great pride in presiding over his family and has rigid ideas about the way each member should behave. He believes that his son Edward should not play with dolls, for example, and he would take any show of independence by a woman as an insult. He is also shocked by homosexuality, as is seen when his friend misinterprets his comments about male friendship and makes a sexual advance. But Clive is also a hypocrite because he wastes no time in seducing Mrs. Saunders and constantly lusts after her. Clive returns briefly at the end of act two to say that he does not feel the same about Betty as he once did.

# Edward

Edward is the nine-year-old son of Clive and Betty, and he is played by a woman. Edward likes dolls, although this displeases both his parents. His father wants him to act like a man, and his mother instructs him not to tell anyone at school that he likes dolls, because then they will not speak to him or let him play cricket. Edward may harbor a secret hatred of his father, because he does nothing to intervene in the last moment of act one, when Joshua is about to shoot Clive.

In act two, Edward is shown as a man in his thirties. He is gay and lives with Gerry. But their relationship breaks up, and he moves in with Lin, Victoria, and Cathy. He is happy doing housework.

# Ellen

Ellen is the young governess in charge of Edward and Victoria. She is a lesbian and falls in love with Betty.

# Gerry

Gerry is a gay man who lives with Edward. He boasts a lot about his sexual life and conquests.

After a disagreement with Edward about the terms of their relationship, he moves out of the apartment they share. Gerry is later befriended by Betty.

## *Joshua*

Joshua is a black African who is the servant in Clive and Betty's home. He is played by a white man. Joshua has internalized the values of his employers; he hates his own tribe and does not condemn the killing of his parents by the British. He serves his master, Clive, informing him that the stable boys are not to be trusted and then whipping them as Clive instructs. Joshua also reports to Clive on the illicit attraction between Harry and Betty and on Ellen's sexual love for Betty. But he also harbors resentment about his subordinate position, which is suggested by his insulting Betty on two occasions. And in the last moment of act one, Joshua points a gun at Clive and is ready to shoot.

## *Lin*

Lin appears only in act two. A working-class friend of Victoria, she is a divorced mother (of Cathy) and is also a lesbian. Her husband used to beat her, and she says she hates men. Lin is sexually attracted to Victoria, and eventually the two of them live together along with Edward.

## *Martin*

Martin is Victoria's husband in act two. He is a

novelist who claims to be writing a novel about women from the woman's point of view. He prides himself on being in favor of women's liberation and believes that he goes out of the way to make his wife happy, but in fact he gets impatient with her indecisiveness and only serves to confuse her. Victoria believes that she is more intelligent than he is, but she is still dominated by him.

## Maud

Maud is Betty's mother, and she enjoys giving Betty old-fashioned advice about life and love.

## Mrs. Saunders

Mrs. Saunders is an independent-minded widow who comes to the home of Clive and his family for safety after the local Africans become threatening. She is seduced by Clive, though she does not like him. She does, however, enjoy the pleasures of sex.

## Victoria

Victoria is the daughter of Clive and Betty. In act one, she is two years old and is represented only by a doll. In act two, she is married to Martin and has a child, Tommy. Victoria, who reads widely and likes to offer her intellectual insights to her less educated friend Lin, is in a dilemma about whether she should accept a job as a teacher in Manchester that would separate her from her husband. Since she is beginning to assert herself and not be so subordinate to Martin, she eventually decides to take the job. She also experiments with bisexuality, embarking on a sexual affair with Lin. Victoria does not get along with her mother, remarking that after a ten-minute conversation with Betty she needs to take a two-hour bath to get over it.

## *Colonialism and Sexism*

Churchill wrote in her introduction to the play that she wanted to show "the parallel between colonial and sexual oppression." She meant that it is the same mentality of the colonial power, reflecting male values, that also results in the oppression of women.

The colonial attitude can be seen in Clive, who has contempt for those he refers to as the "natives." His attitude is paternalistic. He thinks of himself as a father to the natives, just as he is a father to his family. He also has a low opinion of the natives' capabilities. After praising his black servant, Joshua, as a jewel, he adds, "You'd hardly notice that the fellow's black." Clive regards the local African population as little better than savages, commenting that he knows three different tribal leaders who "would all gladly chop off each other's heads and wear them round their waists." He exerts harsh discipline on the black stable boys when he learns that they cannot be trusted to be loyal servants of his interests.

The point Churchill wishes to make is that Joshua, the only black man in the play, has internalized the values of his white colonial masters and therefore cooperates in his own oppression. As he says at the beginning of the play, "My skin is black but oh my soul is white." His goal is to become what white men want him to be; he says he lives only for his master, a comment that clearly echoes the way Clive's wife Betty regards her own life.

Betty's own attitude contributes to a sexism that pervades the play, especially in act one. Men such as Clive and Harry Bagley go out and have adventures, but the women (Betty, Maud, Ellen) lead dull, monotonous lives. Betty's place is in the home, reading poetry, playing the piano, and waiting for Clive, around whom her life revolves, to return. Gender roles are clearly defined, and the women accept them as part of the nature of things. "The men have their duties and we have ours," says Maud, and Betty regards her own loneliness as a form of service not only to her husband but also to the British Empire. She believes that she is perfectly happy, although she has little understanding of what her true nature and capabilities might be. She has allowed herself to be formed entirely to fit a male image of what a woman should be.

The men have very patronizing ideas about women. Clive regards his wife, and most likely all women, as delicate, sensitive creatures given to fainting and hysteria. But he may prefer things this way, since the weakness of women enables him to feel strong and chivalrous. He regards any sign of independence in a woman as an insult; it is he who must be the protector. Similarly, Harry, when he declares his love for Betty, reserves for himself the active life and allocates to her a purely passive role:

"I need you, and I need you where you are, I need you to be Clive's wife. I need to go up rivers and know you are sitting here thinking of me."

## **Topics for Further Study**

- Are there innate differences between men and women, in terms of their interest in or aptitude for certain careers or leisure pursuits, or are most differences a result of social conditioning? Do research to learn what experts have to say on this question. What are some of the ways in which social conditioning is changing today?

- To what extent is being gay considered acceptable in America today and to what extent is there still prejudice and discrimination against gays? What forms does that discrimination take? Should laws be passed to make discrimination against gays illegal?

- Is homosexuality innate, or is it a learned behavior? In other words, are people born gay, or do they choose to be gay? Investigate the current research on this question.

- In order to succeed and be accepted in American society, do blacks have to "act white" (like Joshua in the play)? Explain your answer.

---

The sexism of the men extends to other areas. In act one, scene two, Ellen and Betty begin to play catch, and the men express surprise and congratulations whenever the women manage to catch the ball. Obviously, women are not expected to possess such an ability. Then Edward, who is only nine years old but has learned well from his father, tells his mother, and then Ellen, that they shouldn't play ball because they cannot catch. It is a judgment that Betty is all too ready to agree with. Then the men take over. Edward cannot catch and is mocked by Harry and Clive; it appears that this is a test of masculinity. And when Betty informs Clive that he has hurt Edward's feelings, Clive reveals another of his unconscious gender stereotypes: "A boy has no business having feelings."

The aim of the play is to deconstruct these gender stereotypes. Edward, for example, although a boy, likes to play with dolls, even though he is told by his elders that such behavior is not considered masculine. The playwright invites the audience to question this and other assumptions, such as the passivity of women. Mrs. Saunders, for example, shows that a woman can enjoy sex for its own sake, just as a man may, and this is in contrast to Betty's dreamy, romantic notions of love.

The theme of liberation from the false, socially induced constraints of gender becomes even more pronounced in act two, which shows how the characters, especially Betty and Edward, break free of the rigid roles that were formerly prescribed for them. Society has changed, too, making it easier for them to do so. Betty is able to acquire a real job of her own, and she also relearns the pleasures of auto-eroticism, initially as an act of rebellion against her husband and her mother. Betty's discovery shows how women are now more able to accept their bodies and sexual desires as natural, not something to be ashamed of or repressed. This theme is also apparent in act two, scene three, when Victoria and Lin chant in praise of ancient female goddesses.

In addition to the liberation of women, in the world portrayed in act two, homosexuality is not the shameful thing it was to Clive or Harry. Edward and Gerry can live as an openly gay couple, and Betty is not distressed at her knowledge that her son is gay or that her daughter is involved in a sexual relationship with her girlfriend, Lin.

There are changes in the way the family is constructed, too. If act one is a satire on the

Victorian family, in which desires and sexual orientation are repressed in order to present a false appearance, act two shows the forming of alternative family structures. For example, a gay man, Edward, lives with two women and their two children. One of the women, Lin, is a confirmed lesbian, while the other, Victoria, is experimenting with bisexuality. This is a long way from the image of the family that Clive presents in the first scene of the play.

Churchill also sets out to undermine the ideology of colonialism. Since such a system is based on exploitation, violence, and the belief in the inferiority of the colonized people, it can only result in resentment and, ultimately, violence, as is apparent several times in the play. Joshua, for example, for all his dutiful attempts to act as his master wants him to, brazenly defies Betty's orders (which also reveals the powerless position of women). When Joshua aims a gun at Clive's head in the final scene in act one, it hardly comes as a surprise. Whatever surface appearances might suggest, Joshua will never wholly succeed in becoming "white." (The specter of colonialism returns in act two, when Lin's brother, Bill, a British soldier, is killed in Northern Ireland, where the British are fighting a guerrilla war against Irish nationalists. This time the emphasis is on the dispiriting life led by the soldiers who serve in the British army, which the Irish nationalists believe to be the arm of a colonizing, oppressive power.)

# Style

## *Gender Reversals*

The play uses a number of unconventional techniques to create its effects. One of these is for some of the characters to be played by actors of the opposite gender. This reinforces the theme of undermining gender stereotyping. For example, Edward as a nine-year-old boy is played by a woman, which visually reinforces for the audience the notion that Edward does not behave in the way his Victorian family believes a boy should. Betty is played by a man because, as Churchill states in her introduction to the play, "she wants to be what men want her to be." She does not value herself as a woman. Her true nature is therefore hidden from herself and others. Joshua is played by a white man, to reinforce the idea that he has embraced the values of white culture and behaves as his white employers expect of him.

In act two, the characters are played for the most part by members of their own gender. Betty is now played by a woman, which visually reinforces for the audience the fact that for the first time she is discovering who she really is. Edward is played by a man, to show that he has found his own identity and is comfortable with being gay.

The only exception to this is that four-year-old Cathy is played by a man. This has the same effect as the playing of Edward by a woman in act one. It subverts traditional expectations of how a girl should behave and what interests she should have. Cathy, for example, likes to play rough games with the boys, and she also plays with a toy gun. The other reason for having Cathy played by a man is, as Churchill writes, "because the size and presence of a man on stage seemed appropriate to the emotional force of young children."

## *Structure*

Another unconventional technique in the play is the use in act two of many of the same characters from act one, even though the action takes place one hundred years later. Churchill managed this by having the characters age only twenty-five years from act one to act two.

The two acts are different in other ways, too. The first is dominated by men, especially Clive, who tries hard to keep everything under control, arranged the way he believes things should be. But the second act is dominated more by the women and the gays, who show a capacity for change and a willingness to entertain new ways of being and living. Those who were powerless earlier—Betty in particular—now grow into positions in which they feel more in control of their destinies. The fact that when the play was first staged the actor who played Clive in act one also played the child Cathy in act two reinforces this idea of the reversals that have taken place—the powerlessness of the old ideals in a new world. (Churchill wrote the play for seven actors, which means that some parts must be doubled. It is not essential, however, that Clive be doubled with Cathy; other combinations are possible.) In act two it is the man, Martin, the equivalent of Clive in act one, who must struggle to come to terms with the new feminist consciousness rather than have everything his own way.

Another way in which the structure of the play allows the playwright to convey her themes occurs at the end of act one. The final scene appears to have the form of a typical romantic comedy. Enemies are banished, order is restored, love triumphs, and there is a wedding celebration for the happy couple. Clive appears to sum things up when he makes a speech in neatly rhymed verse that ends, "All murmuring of discontent is stilled. / Long may you live in peace and joy and bliss." But, of course, the reality is somewhat different. Not only is there a nasty little quarrel about the doll, as a result of which Clive hits his son, but there is also the more fundamental fact that all the words in praise of the marriage and in celebration of the ending of discontent are false. Nothing is what it appears, since Ellen and Harry are in fact gay and are marrying merely to shore up appearances, and a drunken Joshua is about to take a shot at Clive. The ostensibly comic form is belied by the reality of the situation.

## *Women's Liberation Movement*

Britain in the 1970s was marked by vigorous and politically effective campaigns for women's rights and gay rights. The First National Women's Liberation Conference was held in Oxford in 1970. The goals it decided upon were equal pay for women, equal opportunity in education and employment, abortion rights, day care, and free contraception. The women's liberation movement aimed to raise women's consciousness about social issues and encouraged them to challenge some of the basic underpinnings of a male-dominated society—the assumption that women should always be secondary to men, for example, or that women are important only through their relationships with men. Women increasingly challenged the traditional division of labor in the family and in the workplace. They rejected the idea that certain roles, such as child-rearing and housekeeping, were suited only to women, and they fought for the right to pursue careers in areas traditionally open only to men. They argued that traditional gender roles had been constructed by a male-dominated society rather than being inherent in the nature of human life. And what had been socially constructed could also be changed.

During this time, there was a feeling of

excitement among many women that a new era was dawning. Gillian Hanna, one of the founders of the feminist theatre company Monstrous Regiment, recollected:

> We wanted to change the world. At the time, this didn't seem like such an outrageous project. All around us, women in every area of the world we knew were doing the same thing. It seemed as natural as breathing.

The women's movement made a measurable impact on 1970s British society. The Equal Pay Act of 1970, which was implemented in 1975, established the principle of equal pay for equal work. In 1975, the Sex Discrimination Act banned discrimination on the grounds of gender or marital status and established the Equal Opportunities Commission. Women also gained the right to maternity leave.

# Compare & Contrast

- **1880**: The British Empire is at the height of its power. More than a quarter of the world's land-mass is under British rule, including large portions of Africa.

  **1980**: Britain has long since renounced its empire and is now a middle-sized European power and a member of the European

Community (EC). There is an ongoing debate in Britain about how much national sovereignty should be surrendered to an EC bureaucracy.

**Today**: Britain's colonial legacy is apparent in the sometimes troubled relations between the races in what is now a multi-ethnic nation. The majority of non-white Britons are descendents of Asian or West Indian immigrants (former subjects of the British Empire) who were admitted to Britain beginning in the 1950s. In 2001, race riots erupt in three northern English cities.

- **1880**: In Britain, women are not allowed to vote, and educational opportunities are limited. In the better-off families, a woman's place is in the home, supervising the large household and entertaining visitors. Only working-class women take paid employment, in the textile industry, for example, or as domestic help.

  **1980**: The women's movement is a powerful force in British society, and discrimination by gender or marital status is illegal. Britain has its first woman prime minister, Margaret Thatcher, and the number of women in the professions increases, as does the number of women in the workforce as a whole. But women's earnings. still lag behind those of men.

**Today**: Economic inequalities between men and women remain. In Britain, women's earnings are only 81 percent of men's. Women still face obstacles to career success, including the so-called glass ceiling (a barrier that is invisible but is nonetheless there), which make it difficult for women to be promoted to the highest levels in business.

- **1880**: The growing suffragette movement, with its aim of securing voting rights for women and access to the professions, helps to bring more women into work in the theater. Many actresses play important roles in producing and performing plays.

**1980**: As a result of the women's liberation movement of the 1970s, an impressive number of plays are written and produced by women, many of which dramatize issues that are important in the lives of women.

**Today**: Young women playwrights now start writing, confident of their equal status with men. But women involved in British theater also say that women need to have greater access to money and resources, that there should be more women in positions of power in theater management, and that more plays by women should be produced in large theaters.

# Gay Liberation Movement

A major landmark in the acceptance of homosexuality in Britain was the Sexual Offences Act of 1967, which decriminalized homosexuality between consenting adults in private. The age of consent was fixed at twenty-one, five years older than the age of consent for heterosexual acts. (In 1994, the age of consent for homosexual acts was lowered to eighteen.) But gay people still faced discrimination, such as being fired from their jobs or denied custody of their children. In 1970, the Gay Liberation Front (GLF) was formed. That year, the first gay rights demonstration in Britain took place in London. More than one hundred members of the GLF protested police harassment and intimidation. The first Gay Pride march was held in London in 1972, and a newspaper, *Gay News,* was published from 1972 to 1983. Adapting a slogan from the American civil rights movement ("black is beautiful"), gays proclaimed that "gay is good." They rejected the shame and guilt that had often accompanied gay life in the past, due to disapproval of homosexuality by church and state and to almost universally negative portrayals of gays in the media.

The GLF also organized radical protests involving sit-ins at pubs (the British equivalent of a bar) that refused to serve gays, and GLF activists disrupted a lecture by noted psychiatrist Professor Hans Eysenck after he advocated electric-shock aversion therapy to "cure" homosexuality. The increasing visibility of gay people encouraged many to "come out" and live openly (as Edward and Gerry do in *Cloud Nine),* without having to disguise the fact that they were gay. Many gays (as well as feminists) linked their oppression to the structure of the traditional family. By learning to form nontraditional family structures, many gays declared that they had rejected the masculine and feminine roles that society had designed for them. During this period, gays became freer in discussing the ways in which a masculine identity had been imposed on them in their upbringing although such an identity did not correspond to what they felt themselves to be (just as in the play, Edward comes to realize that the kind of man his father expected him to become was not who he was).

## Women's and Gay Theater

The 1970s saw the emergence of feminist and gay theater in Britain. Cultural historian Michelene Wandor, in *Carry On, Understudies,* divides this period into four phases. From 1969 to 1973, avant-garde and experimental writing flourished, and street theater companies performed plays that probed social issues from a socialist and feminist viewpoint. Theater was viewed as a means of raising women's social consciousness. Phase two was from 1973 to 1977, during which alternative theater gained some stability as a result of receiving state subsidies. This was the period when women's professional theater companies, dedicated to producing work by women or emphasizing women's issues, began to spring up. The most prominent of these were the Women's Theatre Group (1974) and Monstrous Regiment (1975-76). Churchill became involved in Monstrous Regiment and wrote her play *Vinegar Tom* for the company. During the same period, Gay Sweatshop, a theater company made up of lesbians and gay men, was also formed. Phase three, from 1977 onward, was a period of contraction for alternative theater groups, as the Arts Council reduced its subsidies. Phase four, according to Wandor, was from 1979 onward, when numerous female and gay playwrights came to prominence. These were either new writers with confident voices as a result of the work done by others over the previous decade or experienced writers who had worked through the previous stages and developed a stronger theatrical voice. These writers included, in addition to Churchill and Wandor herself, Pam Gems, Mary O'Malley, Nell Dunn, and Claire Luckham.

# Critical Overview

When *Cloud Nine* was first produced in England in 1979, it was a commercial success, establishing Churchill as a leading British playwright. However, critics were divided as to the merits of the play. Robert Cushman in the *Observer*(quoted in *Plays in Review)* described the second act as "almost the best thing to arrive in the London theatre this young and dismal year." And John Barber's verdict in the *Daily Telegraph*(quoted by Erica Beth Weintraub in *Dictionary of Literary Biography)* was also positive; Barber described it as "cheerfully entangling itself in the problems of fitting complex human instincts into workable social patterns." But a different view was taken by J. C. Trewin of the *Birmingham Post,* who expressed puzzlement about the play's themes. Whether the play was "a treatise on bisexuality" or "a view of parents and children," Trewin regarded it as "superfluous." He argued that the satirical approach to the British Empire in the first act was a hackneyed theme, and he dubbed the second act a "wholly muddled fantasy." Peter Jenkins, in the *Spectator*(quoted in *Plays in Review),* was also less than enthusiastic, writing that the play's "most constant danger is degeneration into a mere sequence of acting exercises, or cabaret turns, loosely plotted together."

When the play reached New York in 1981, critics were lavish with their praise. Rex Reed, in the *New York Times,* called it "the most rewarding surprise of the theatrical season," and Clive Barnes in the *New York Post* wrote that it is "a play that has something to say about kindness, affection, perversion, and most of all love" (both reviews quoted by Weintraub).

Scholars of the theater continue to write about the themes and techniques of the play, which has acquired a permanent place in the history of British theater.

# What Do I Read Next?

- *Rites*(1970), by British playwright Maureen Duffy, is an imaginative recasting of *The Bacchae,* a play by the ancient Greek dramatist Euripides. Like *Cloud Nine,* it is a feminist play that brings traditional gender roles into question.

- Wendy Wasserstein is a leading

American playwright; her play *The Heidi Chronicles*(1988) is a satirical approach to the successes and failures of two decades of the feminist movement.

- Churchill's *Plays Two*(1990) contains four of her best plays: *Softcops, Top Girls, Fen,* and *Serious Money.* Churchill's introduction and her notes on each play provide an illuminating commentary.

- Elaine Aston's *An Introduction to Feminism and Theatre*(1994) is a lucid introduction that explains difficult theoretical issues in a way that a reader new to the field can understand.

## Sources

Aston, Elaine, *Caryl Churchill*, Northcote House, 1997, pp. 31–37.

Churchill, Caryl, *Cloud Nine*, in *Plays*, Methuen, 1985, pp. 245–320.

Fanon, Frantz, *Black Skins, White Masks*, Grove Press, 1967.

Lloyd Evans, Gareth, and Barbara Lloyd Evans, *Plays in Review, 1956–1980: British Drama and the Critics*, Batsford Academic and Educational, 1985, pp. 235–36.

Millett, Kate, *Sexual Politics*, Virago, 1977.

Wandor, Michelene, *Carry On, Understudies: Theatre and Sexual Politics*, Routledge & Kegan Paul, 1986.

Weintraub, Erica Beth, "Caryl Churchill," in *Dictionary of Literary Biography*, Vol. 13: *British Dramatists Since World War II*, edited by Stanley Weintraub, Gale Research, 1982, pp.118–24.

# Further Reading

Betsko, Kathleen, and Rachel Koenig, *Interviews with Contemporary Women Playwrights,* William Morrow, 1987, pp. 75–84.

> In this interview, Churchill talks about her work, including *Cloud Nine, Top Girls, Fen,* and other plays.

Gray, Francis, "Mirrors of Utopia: Caryl Churchill and Joint Stock," in *British and Irish Drama since 1960,* edited by James Acheson, St. Martin's, 1993, pp. 47–59.

> Gray examines the far-reaching consequences of the plays that emerged from Churchill's work with the Joint Stock Company, which added a political dimension to her work. He includes an analysis of *Cloud Nine.*

Itzin, Catherine, *Stages in the Revolution: Political Theatre in Britain since 1968,* Eyre Methuen, 1980.

> This is a year-by-year account of the development of what Itzen calls the theater of political change from 1968 to 1978. She includes sections on Churchill and the important women's companies of the period as well as other companies that gave

opportunities to women writers and performers.

Wandor, Michelene, *Drama Today: A Critical Guide to British Drama, 1970-1990,* Longman, 1993.

This is a concise guide to themes, writers, and works in contemporary British drama. Wandor discusses Churchill along with Nell Dunn, Harold Pinter, Edward Bond, Alan Ayckbourn, and others.